THE VOCAL LIBRARY HIGH VOICE

Class

Concert Arrangements by
Richard Walters

To access companion recorded performances
and piano accompaniments online, visit:
**www.halleonard.com/mylibrary**

Enter Code
7596-4933-7268-7127

On the cover: John Henry Twachtman, *Icebound*, c. 1889, oil on canvas, 25¹/₄ x 30¹/₄ inches, Friends of American Art Collection, 1917.200, © 1992 The Art Institute of Chicago.

ISBN: 978-0-7935-1844-9

7777 W. BLUEMOUND RD. P.O. BOX 13819 MILWAUKEE, WI 53213



Visit Hal Leonard Online at
**www.halleonard.com**

# Contents

*for solo voice and piano, unless otherwise noted*



On the recording
* Martha Cares, soprano
** Steven Stolen, tenor
*** Duet
Richard Walters, piano
Rebecca Price Arrensen, flute
Larry Shapiro, violin

Recorded 5/92 at Aire Born Studios, Indianapolis
Richard Walters, producer

The price of this publication includes access to companion recorded performances and piano accompaniments online, for download or streaming, using the unique code found on the title page.
Visit **www.halleonard.com/mylibrary** and enter the access code.

# ON THE RECORDING

MARTHA CARES, soprano, is a performer of uncommon versatility. Her opera career includes some twenty roles, which she has performed with several companies, highlighted by Susanna, Musetta, Gretel, Lauretta, Papagena, and Zerlina. For two years she was in residence at the Lyric Center for American Artists, affiliated with Lyric Opera of Chicago, and also spent a season as a resident young artist with Greater Miami Opera. In addition to her work in opera and concert, she has a successful career recording commercials for television and radio. Ms. Cares is also featured on the Hal Leonard album "Popular Ballads for Classical Singers."

STEVEN STOLEN, tenor, is in high demand in the field of concert and oratorio, specializing particularly in distinguished performances of Baroque music. He has appeared with many American orchestras and chamber orchestras, and has won several awards and competitions, highlighted by the Erwin Bodky International Competition held at the Boston Early Music Festival. Mr. Stolen is a frequent and acclaimed recitalist with a deep and varied repertory, and has appeared in two dozen opera roles, including the title roles in *Albert Herring* and *The Student Prince*. He also may be heard on the Hal Leonard albums "The Classical Singer's Christmas Album" and "Popular Ballads for Classical Singers."

RICHARD WALTERS, arranger and pianist, is a composer who specializes in writing music for the voice. His principal composition studies were with Dominick Argento. He is managing editor of the concert music division at Hal Leonard Publishing, and develops and oversees a wide variety of publications in his position. Mr. Walters has great versatility as a musician, and besides arranging and composition has worked as a classical and popular pianist, musical coach for opera and musical theatre, stage director, music critic, author, recording producer, commercial music arranger, and orchestrator. More Walters arrangements for voice may be found in the Hal Leonard collections "Popular Ballads for Classical Singers" and "The Classical Singer's Christmas Album."

# I Saw Three Ships



Traditional Irish Carol
Arranged by Richard Walters

2. And what was in those ships all three? On Christ - mas Day, on
Christ - mas Day; And what was in those ships all three on Christ - mas Day in the
mor - ning?
3. Our Sav - ior Christ and His la - dy; On Christ - mas Day, on
sim.

Christ - mas Day; our Sav - ior Christ and His la - dy, on Christ - mas Day in the
mor - ning.
p
4. Pray, whith - er sailed those
ships all three, On Christ - mas Day, On Christ - mas Day; Pray whith - er sailed those
p

mf
ships all three, on Christ - mas Day in the mor - ning? 5. O
8va
mf
they sailed in - to Beth - le - hem, On Christ - mas Day, on Christ - mas Day; O
they sailed in - to Beth - le - hem on Christ - mas Day in the mor - ning.
mp
mf

And
all the bells on earth shall ring, On Christ - mas Day, on Christ - mas Day;
And all the bells on
earth shall ring,
opt.
f
8

*This phrase and the chord after it might also remain forte.

# Wexford Carol

Traditional Irish Carol
Arranged by Richard Walters

Christ-mas Day; In Beth-le-hem up-on that morn There
was a bless-ed Mes-si-ah born. The
p
mf
night be-fore that hap-py tide The no-ble Vir-gin
mp
and her guide Were long time _ seek-ing up and down To

find a lodg - ing in the town. But mark how all ___ things
came to pass; From ___ ev - 'ry door ___ re - pelled, a - las! As
long fore - told, their re - fuge all Was but a hum - - ble
ox - en stall.
3
pp

Near Beth - le - hem did shep - herds keep Their
mp
flocks of lambs _ and feed - ing sheep; To whom God's _ an - gels
did ap - pear, Which put the shep - herds in great fear. "Pre -
pare and go," _ the an - gels said, "To _ Beth - le - hem, _ be
3

not a - fraid; For there you'll find, this hap - py morn, A
princе-ly babe, sweet Je - sus born."
p
With thank - ful heart and
mf
joy - ful mind The shep - herds went the babe to find, And

as God's an - gel had fore - told, They did our Sa - vior
Slower
Christ be - hold. With in a man - ger he was laid, And
pp
by his side the virgin maid,
rit.
vir - gin maid,
a tempo (Slower)
At - tend - ing on the
rit.
mp
Lord of life, Who came on earth to end all strife.
rit.
rit.

# Les anges dans nos campagnes

19th Century French Carol
Arranged by Richard Walters

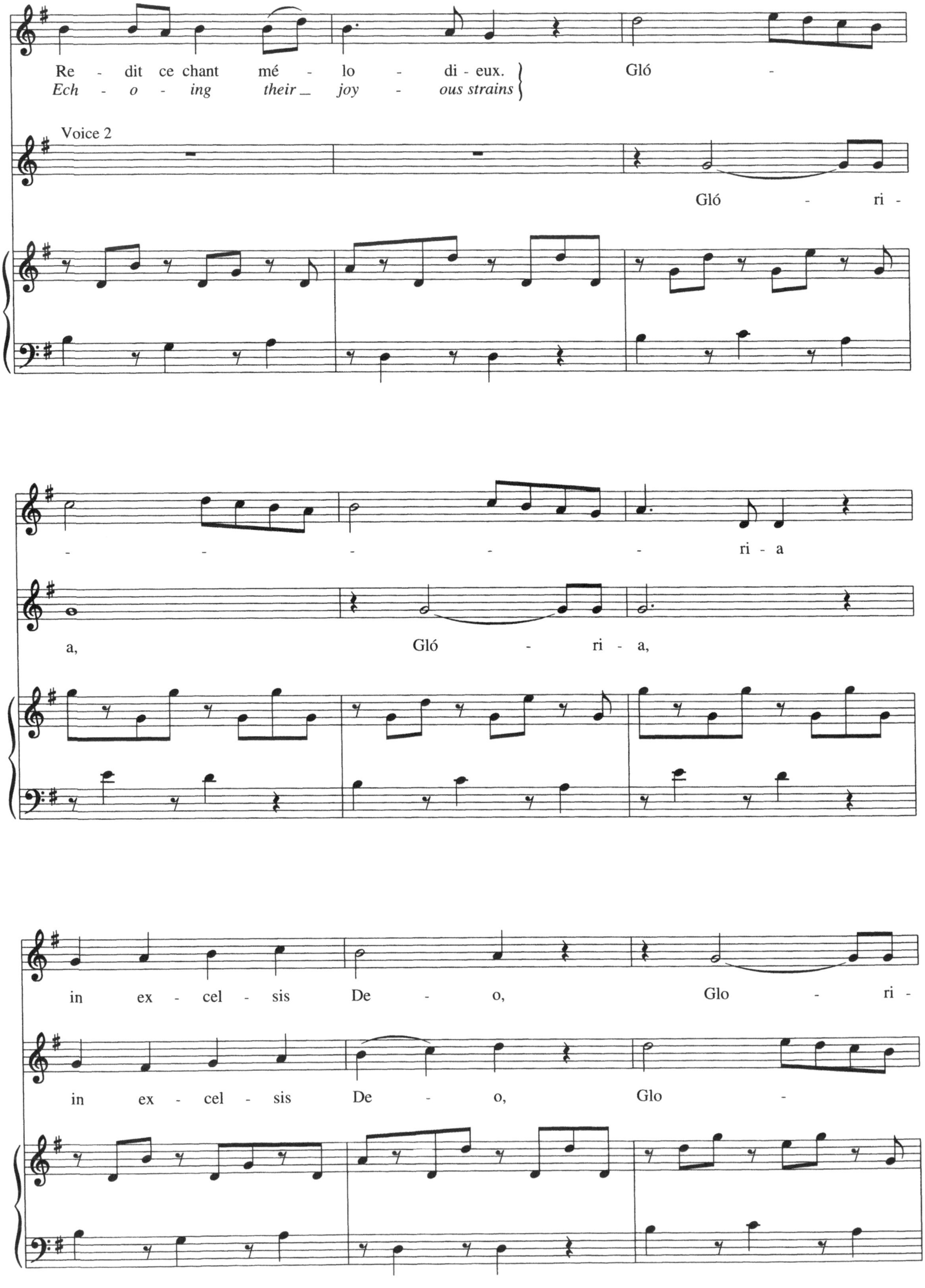

Re - dit ce chant mé - lo - di - eux. Gló -
*Ech - o - ing their _ joy - ous strains*

Voice 2

Gló - ri -

- - - - - ri - a

a, Gló - ri - a,

a,
Gló - ri - a,
ri - a,

in ex - cel - sis De - o.
in ex - cel - sis De - o.

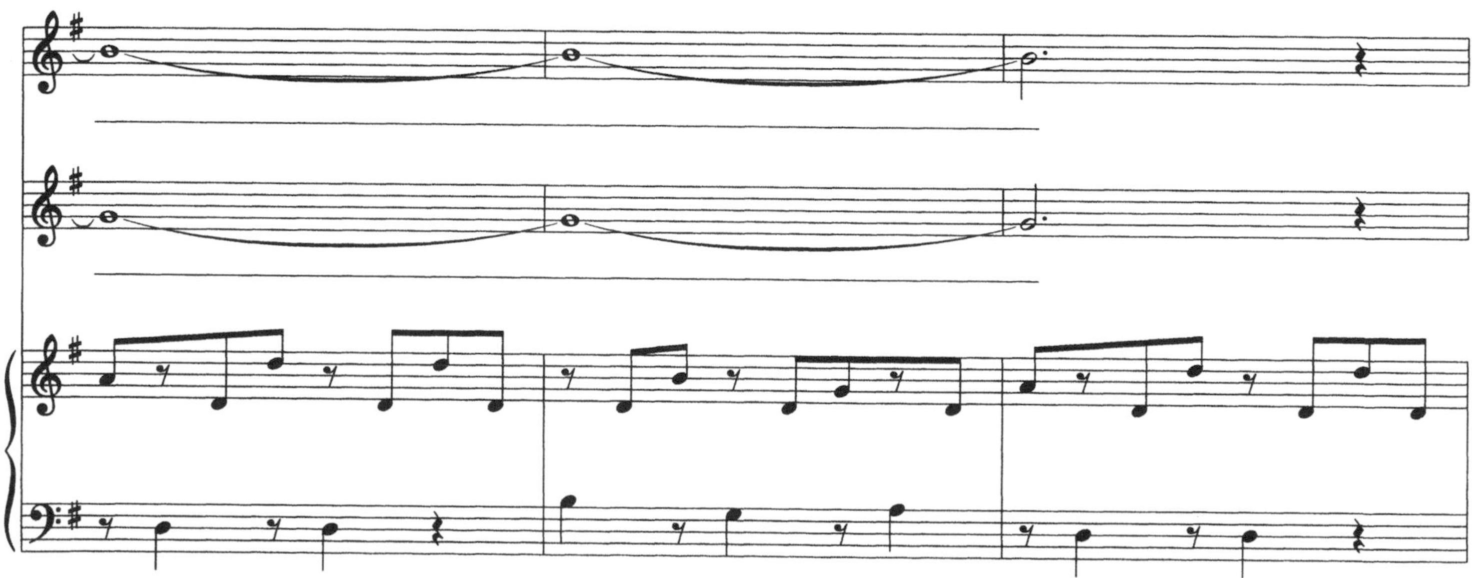

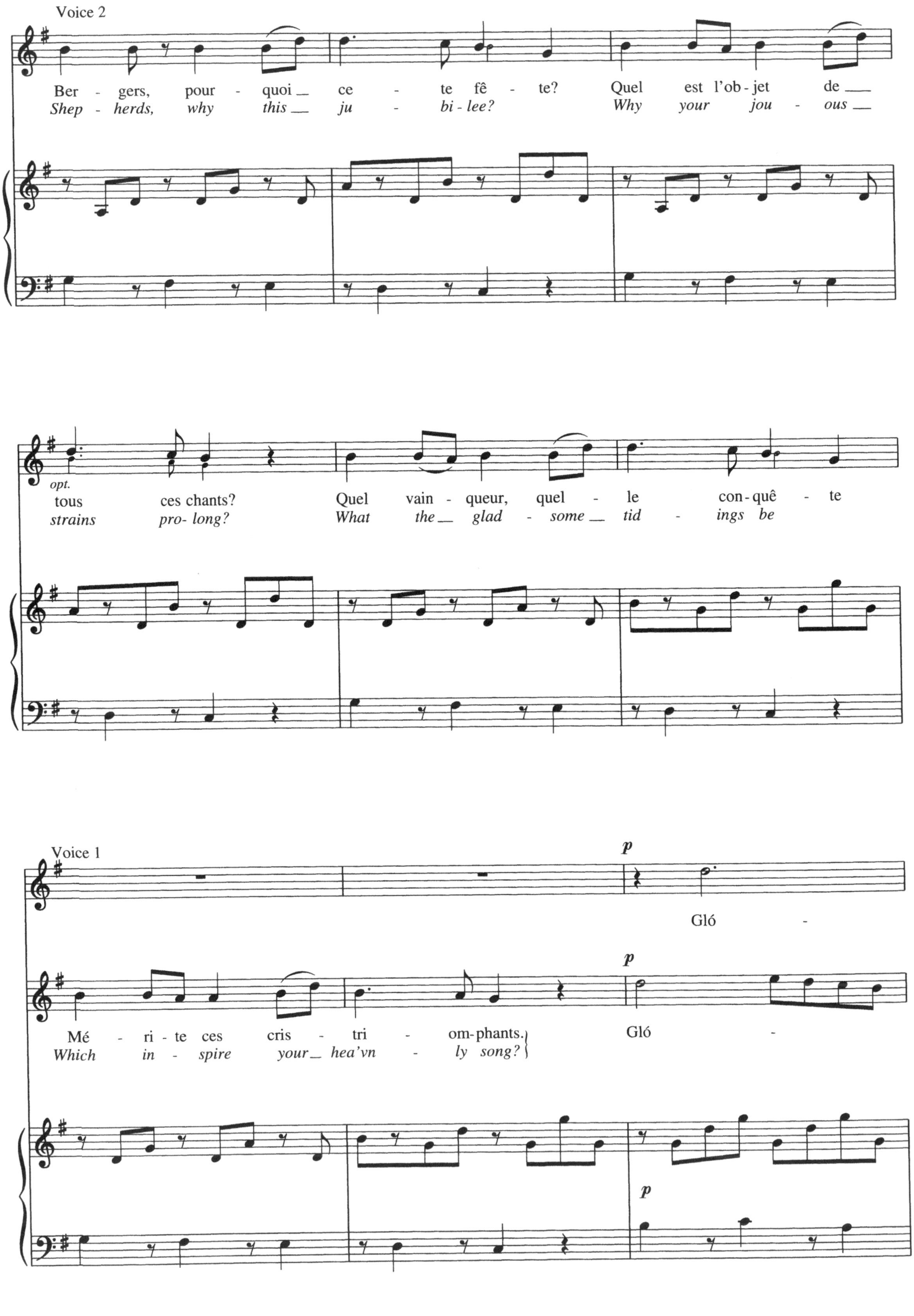
Voice 2
Ber - gers, pour - quoi ce - te fê - te? Quel est l'ob - jet de
Shep - herds, why this ju - bi - lee? Why your jou - ous
opt.
tous ces chants? Quel vain - queur, quel - le con - quê - te
strains pro - long? What the glad - some tid - ings be
Voice 1
p
Gló -
p
Mé - ri - te ces cris - tri - om - phants. Gló -
Which in - spire your hea'vn - ly song?
p

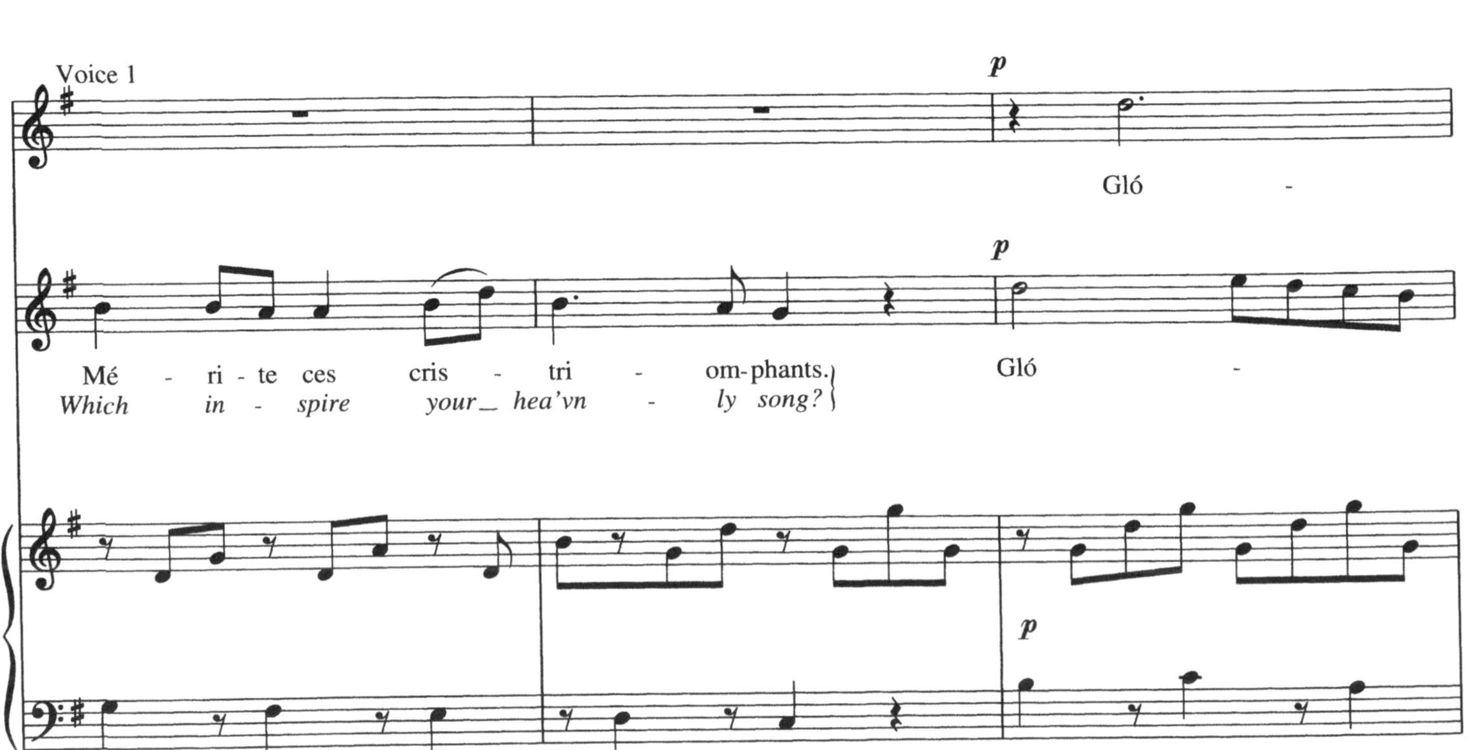

- - - - - - ri - a,
- - - - - ri - a,
pp
in ex - cel - sis De - o. Gló -
mf
pp
in ex - cel - sis De - o Gló -
mf
pp
mf
- - - - - ri - a,
- - - - - - ri - a,

p
in ex - cel - sis De - o.
p
in ex - cel - sis De - o.
p
cresc.
mf

Ber - gers quit - tez vos re - trai - tes, U - nis - sez vous à
Come to Beth - le - hem and see Him whose birth the
Ber - gers quit - tez vos re - trai - tes, U - nis - sez vous à
Come to Beth - le - hem and see Him whose birth the
mf
leur con-certs, Et que vos ten - dres mu - set - tes
an - gels sing; Come a - dore on bend - ed knee
leur con-certs, Et que vos ten - dres mu - set - tes
an - gels sing; Come a - dore on bend - ed knee
f
Fas - sent re - ten - ir les airs. Gló -
Christ the Lord, the new - born King.
f
Fas - sent re - ten - ir les airs. Gló - ri -
Christ the Lord, the new - born King.
f

- - - - - ri - a,
a, Gló - ri - a,
mp
in ex - cel - sis De - o.
f
Gló - ri -
mp
in ex - cel - sis De - o.
f
Gló -
8
mp
f
a, Gló - ri - a,
- - - - - ri - a,
(8)

mp
in ex - cel - sis De - o.
mp
in ex - cel - sis De - o.
mp

p no rit.

# Lo, How a Rose E'er Blooming

Translation by Theodore Baker, 1894

Traditional German Carol
from *Kölner Gesangbuch,* 1599
Arranged by Richard Walters

**Andante espressivo**

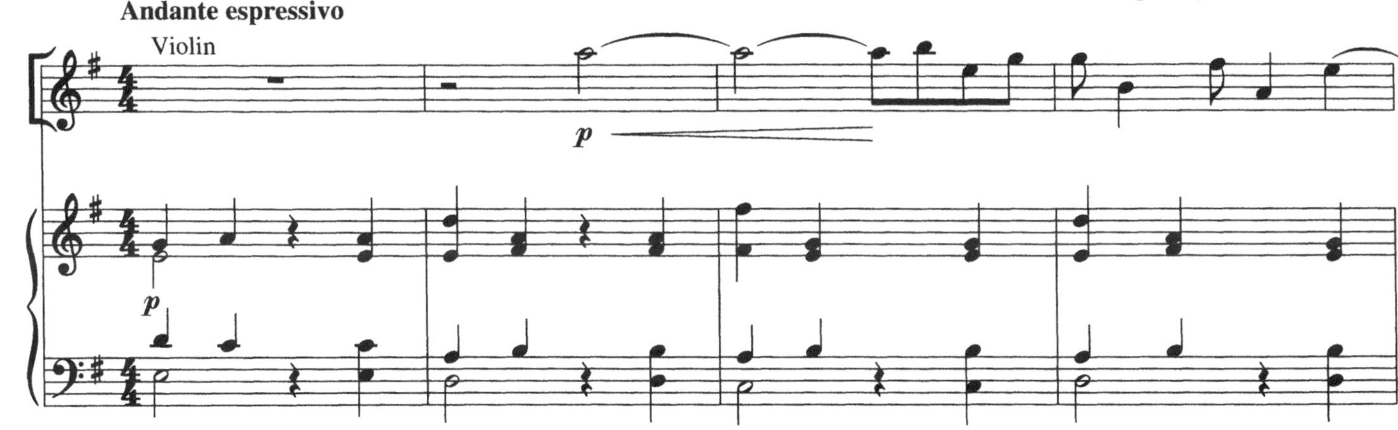

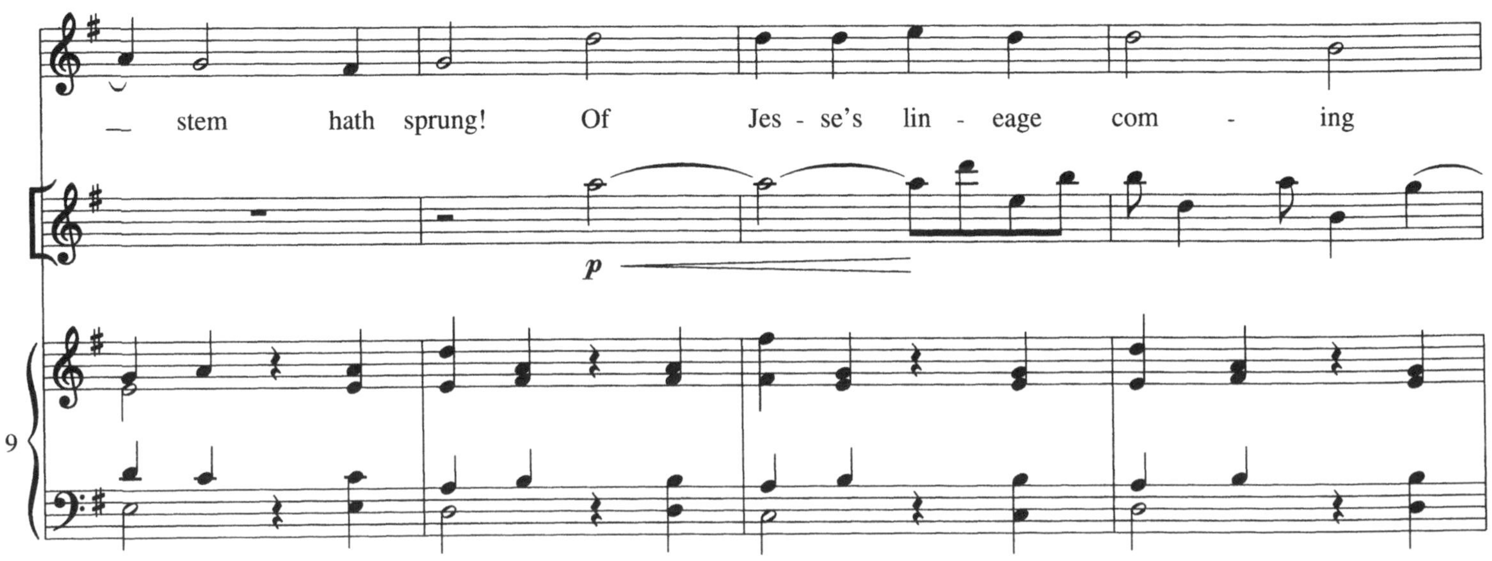

As men of old hath sung.
13
17
It
pp
21
came a flow - 'ret bright, A - mid the cold of win - ter

when half - spent was the night.
p
25
mf
29
mp
I - sa - iah 'twas fore -
told it, The rose I have in mind; With
33

Ma - ry we be - hold it, The vir - gin Mo - ther
37
kind.
41
mp
To show God's love a - right She
45
p

sub. pp
bore to men a sa - vior,
p
pp
49
When half - spent was the night.
p
p
52
rit.
rit.
rit.
56

# Lo, How a Rose E'er Blooming

Translation by Theodore Baker, 1894

Traditional German Carol
from *Kölner Gesangbuch,* 1599
Arranged by Richard Walters

Cut along dotted line.

# The First Noel

Traditional English Carol
Arranged by Richard Walters

No - el,No - el, No - el, No - el,
Born is the King of Is - ra - el.
They look - ed up and saw a star shin-ing
mf
mp
cresc.
mp

in the East beyond them far;
And to the earth it gave great light, And
so it continued both day and night.
cresc.
Noel, Noel, Noel, Noel,

Born is the King of Is - ra -
el.
This star drew
p sub.
nigh to the North - west, O'er Beth - le - hem it
took its rest,
And there it
mp

did both stop and stay Right o - ver the place where
Je - sus lay.
No - el, No -
cresc.
el, No - el, No - el,
Born is the King of Is - ra - el.
f
cresc.
ff

sub. p
Then
let us all with one accord Sing praises

to our heav'n - ly Lord, That
hath made heav'n and earth of naught, And with his
blood man - kind hath bought.
No - el, No - el, No - el, No -
mp

el,
Born is the King of
cresc.
mf
Is - ra - el.
No - el, No -
el No - el, No - el,
opt.
cresc.
Born is the
f

King of Is - ra - el.
p
mf
decresc.
p

# It Came Upon the Midnight Clear

E. H. Sears

Traditional English Melody
Adapted by Arthur Sullivan
Arranged by Richard Walters

heav'n's all gra - cious King!" The world in so - lemn_ still - ness lay To_
8
hear_ the an - gels sing. Still_
(8)
mf
through the clo - ven_ skies they come, With peace - ful wings_un - furled; And_
mp
still their heav'n - ly mu - sic floats O'er_ all_ the wear - y world. A -

bove its sad and low - ly plains They bend on hov - 'ring wing; And
ev - er o'er its Ba - bel sounds, The blessed - ed an - gels sing.
poco rit.
dolce
pp
poco rit.
a tempo
a tempo
More broadly
Yet with the woes of sin and strife The
f
f

world has suf - fered long; Be - neath the an - gel strain have rolled Two _
thou - sand years of wrong; And man, at war with man, hears not The
mf
Slower
pp
love - song which they bring! O hush the noise, ye _ men of strife,
decresc.
pp
And _ hear _ the an - gels sing.
pp

# Un Flambeau, Jeannette, Isabelle

Translated by E. Cuthbert Nunn

17th Century Provençal Carol
Arranged by Richard Walters

11
mf
15
C'est Jé sus, bon - nes gens du ha - meau, Le Christ est né, Ma -
It is Je - sus, good folk of the vil - lage; Christ is born and
18
rie ap - pel - le, Ah! ah! que la mère est
Ma - ry's call - ing, Ah! ah! beau - ti ful is the

bel - le, Ah! ah! ah! que l'En - fant est
Moth - er, Ah! ah! beau - ti - ful is her
mp
21
beau!
son!
mf
24
C'est un tort quand L'En - fant som - meil - le, C'est un tort de cri -
It is wrong when the child is sleep - ing, It is wrong to
mp
mp
28

er si fort.
talk so loud.
mp
31
T'ai - sez - vous, l'un et l'au - tre d'a - bord!
Si - lence, all as you gath - er a - round,
mp
35
pp
Au moin - dre bruit, Jé - sus s'e - veil - le, chut! chut!
Lest your noise should wak - en Je - sus, Hush! hush!
38
pp

Chut! Il dort à mer - veil - le, Chut! chut!
See how fast he slum - bers, Hush! hush!
41
chut! voy - ez comme Il dort!
see how fast He sleeps!
mp
mf
44
rit.
rit.
rit.
47

Slower
Dou - ce - ment dans l'é - ta - ble clo - se, Dou - ce - ment ve -
Soft - ly to the lit - tle sta - ble, Soft - ly for a
p
mp
50
nez un mo - ment! Ap - pro - chez, que Jé - sus est char - mant!
mo - ment come; Look and see how charm - ing is Je - sus,
53
rit.
Comme Il est blanc, comme Il est ro - - se!
How He is soft, His cheeks are ros - - y!
rit.
rit.
56

Slower yet
Do! do! Do! que l'En - fant re - po - se!
Hush! hush! see how the Child is sleep - ing;
59
p
Do! do! do! qu'Il rit en dor - mant.
Hush! hush! see how He smiles in dreams.
p
62
molto rit.
molto rit.
65
molto rit.

# Un Flambeau, Jeannette, Isabelle

Translated by E. Cuthbert Nunn

17th Century Provençal Carol
Arranged by Richard Walters

Cut along dotted line.

# The Holly and the Ivy

Traditional English Carol, c. 1700
Arranged by Richard Walters

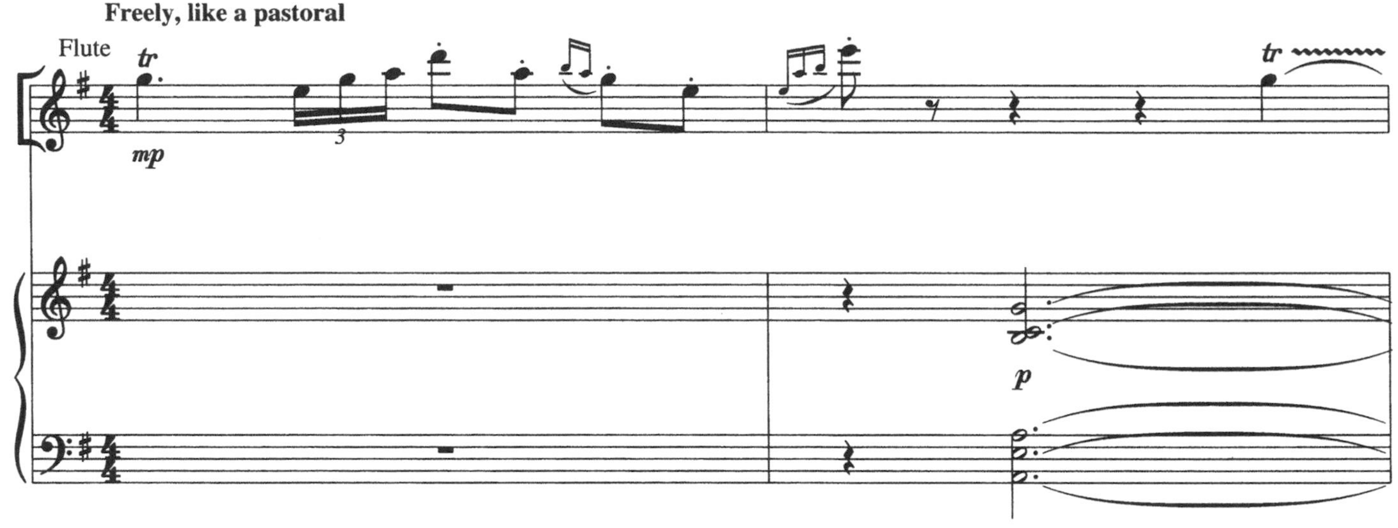

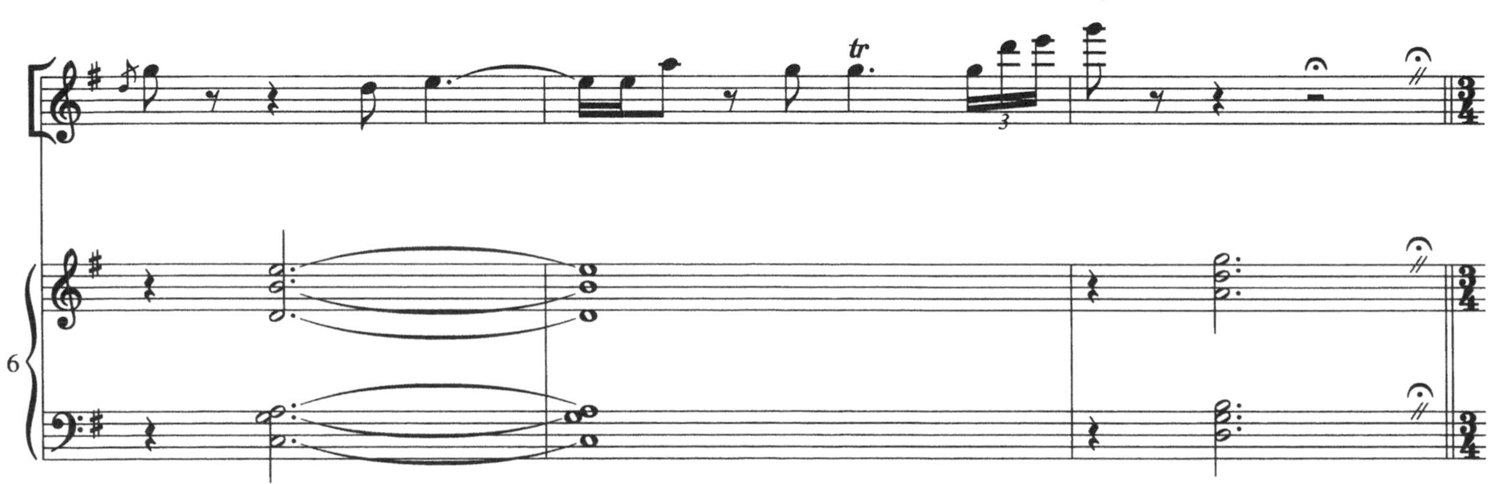

Quick
Voice 2
The hol-ly and the i - vy, When they are both full
mf
sim.
9

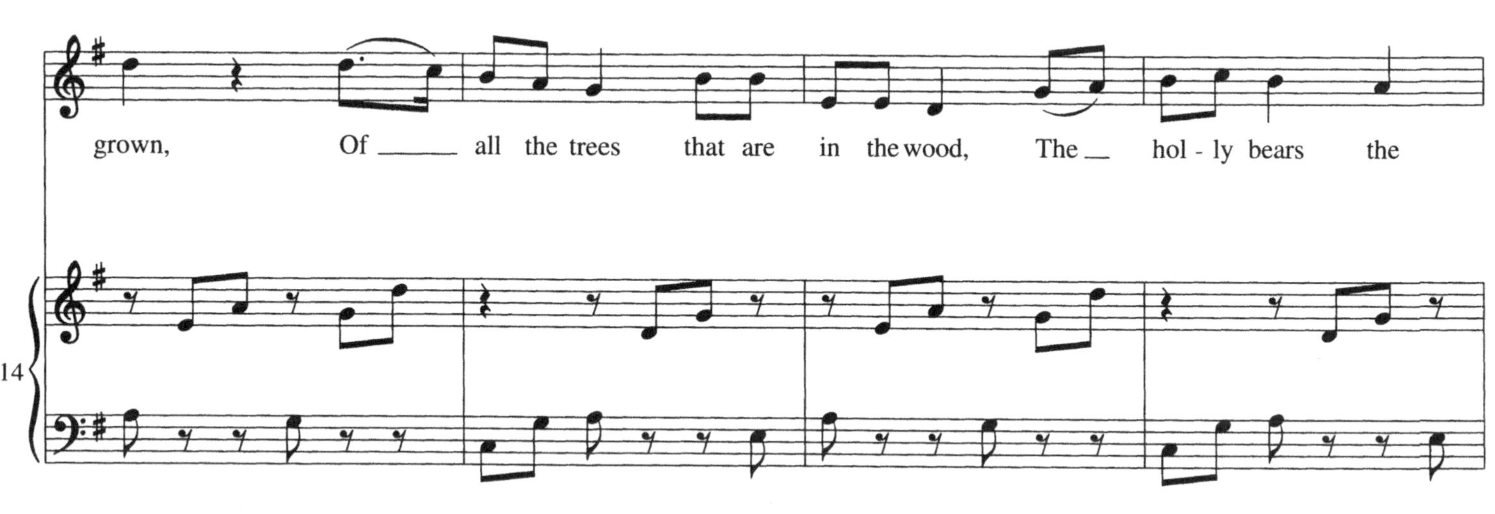
grown, Of all the trees that are in the wood, The hol - ly bears the
14

Voice 1
Oh, the ri - sing of the sun and the run-ning of the
crown.
18

deer. The playing of the merry organ, Sweet singing in the
22
choir.
Voice 2
The holy bears a
Flute
26
Voice 1
And Mary bore sweet
blossom, As white as lily flow'r,
sim.
30

Je - sus Christ to ___ be our dear Sa - vior.
Oh the ris - ing of the sun ___ and the
34
The ___ play - ing of the
Voice 2
run - ning of the deer, The ___ play - ing of the
38

mer - ry or - gan, Sweet sing - ing in the choir.
mer - ry or - gan, Sweet sing - ing in the choir.
41
no rit.
Freely, tempo primo
tr
mp
3
p
45
Quick
Voice 1
The
48
mf

hol - ly bears a ber - ry, As red as an - y blood, And
52
sim.
Ma - ry bore sweet Je - sus Christ to do poor sin - ners good.
Voice 2
Oh, the
56
ris- ing of the sun and the run-ning of the deer, The
60

play-ing of the mer-ry or - gan, Sweet sing-ing in the choir.
64
Voice 1
The hol-ly bears a prick - le, as
Flute
sim.
68
sharp as an - y thorn,
Voice 2
And Ma-ry bore sweet Je-sus Christ on
72

Oh, the ris - ing of the sun and the run - ning of the
Christ - mas Day in the morn.
76
deer, The play - ing of the mer - ry or - gan, Sweet sing - ing in the
The play - ing of the mer - ry or - gan, Sweet sing - ing in the
80

Freely, tempo primo
choir.
choir.
tr
p
84
no rit.
tr
p
mp
88
p
Quick
Voice 1
The
tr
3
91
mf

hol - ly bears a bark as bit - ter as an - y gall, And
Voice 2
The hol - ly bears a bark as bit - ter as an - y
95
sim.
Ma - ry bore sweet Je - sus Christ For to re - deem us all. Oh, the
gall, And Ma - ry bore sweet Je - sus Christ For to re - deem us
99
ris - ing of the sun and the run - ning of the deer, The
all. Oh, the ris - ing of the sun and the run - ning of the
Flute
sim.
103

play-ing of the mer-ry or - gan, Sweet sing-ing in the choir.
deer, The play-ing of the mer-ry or - gan, Sweet sing-ing in the
107
The hol-ly and the i - vy, When they are both full
choir. The hol-ly and the i - vy, When they are both full
8
f
111

grown, Of all the trees that are in the wood, The hol - ly bears the
grown, Of all the trees that are in the wood, The hol - ly bears the
(8)
115
crown. Oh, the ris - ing of the sun and the
crown. Oh, the ris - ing of the sun and the
8
119

run - ning of the deer. The ___ play - ing of the

run - ning of the deer. The ___ play - ing of the

(8) loco

122

rit. molto

mer - ry or - gan, Sweet sing - ing in the choir,

rit. molto

mer - ry or - gan, Sweet sing - ing in the choir,

rit. molto

125

rit. molto

Slow (Tempo primo)
legato
dolce
p
sweet sing - ing, sweet
p legato
sweet sing - ing sweet
128
decresc.
not too slowly p
sing - ing in the choir.
sing - ing in the choir.
tr
p
131

Flute

# The Holly and the Ivy

Traditional English Carol, c. 1700
Arranged by Richard Walters

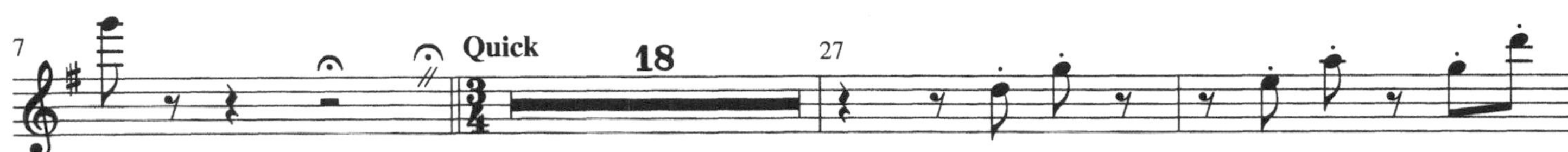


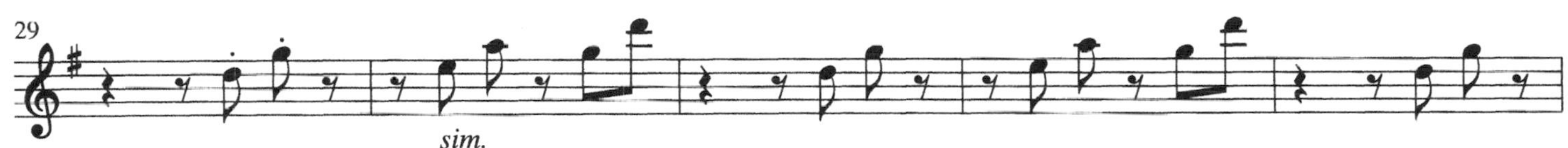

Cut along dotted line.

71
76
81
Freely, tempo primo
tr
87
tr
p
91
tr
3
Quick
10
103
104
sim.
109
8
f
115
(8)
8
121
(8)
loco
127
rit. molto
Slow (tempo primo)
2
tr
p

# Once in Royal David's City

Cecil F. Alexander, 1848

Henry J. Gauntlett, 1858
Arranged by Richard Walters

And His shel - ter was a stable, And His cra - dle
was a stall:
With the poor, and mean, and low - ly
Lived on earth, our Sa - vior ho - ly.
8
(8)

p
sim.
8
(8)
Je - sus is our child - hood's pat - tern, Day by day like
us He grew; He was lit - tle, weak, and help - less,
Tears and smiles like us He knew. And He feel - eth
for our sad - ness, And He shar - eth in our

glad - ness.
cresc.
mf
And our eyes at last shall see Him Thro' His own re -
mf
deem - ing love;
p
For that child so
sub. p
dear and gen - tle Is our Lord in
8

heav'n a - bove.
cresc.
rit.
Broadly
opt.
And He leads His chil - dren on
f
To the place where He has gone.
decresc.
8
p

# Deck the Hall

Old Welsh Carol
Arranged by Richard Walters

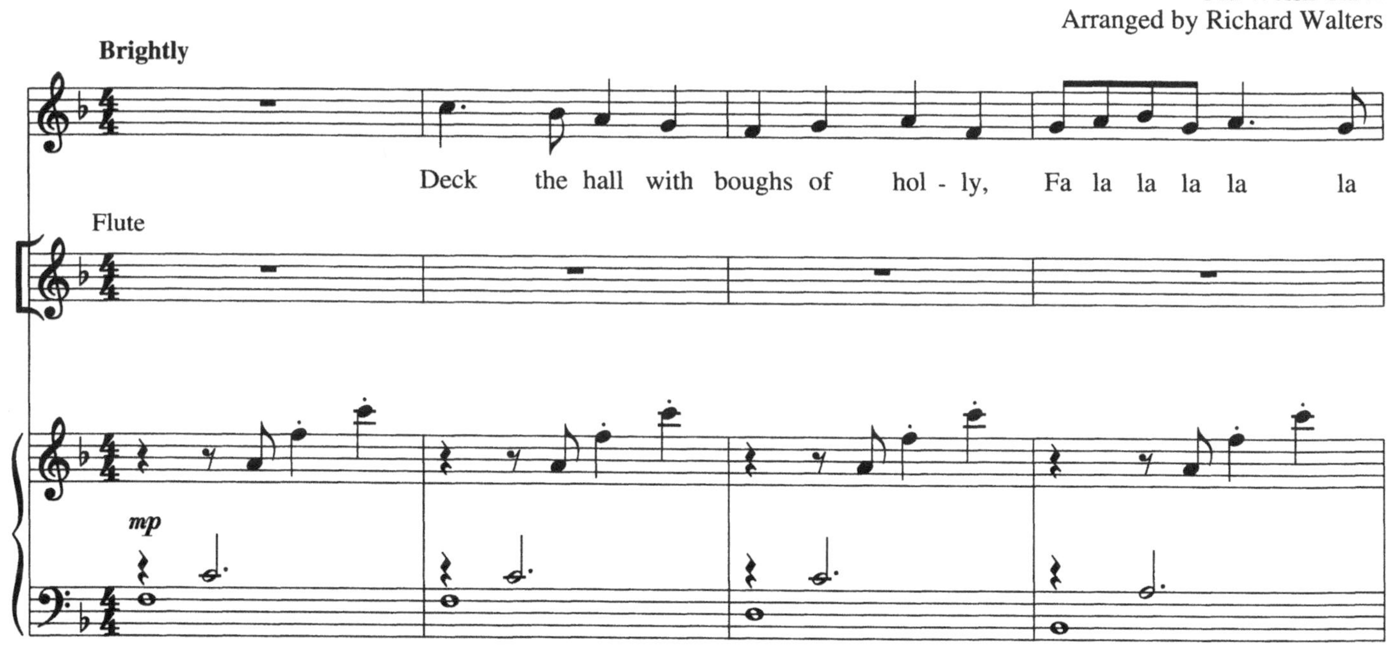

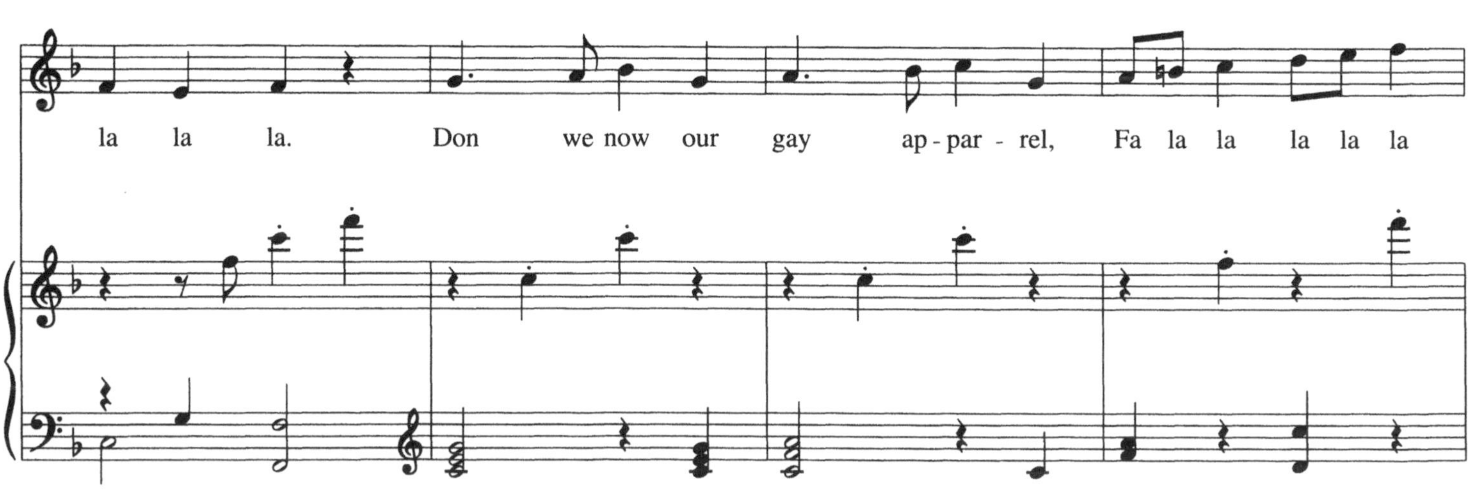

la la la. Troll the an - cient Yule - tide car - ol, Fa la la la la la
8
la la la.
Flute
mf
p
See the blaz - ing Yule be - fore us, Fa la la la la la
p
p

mf
la la la, Strike the harp and join the cho - rus, Fa la la la la la
mf
mf
la la la. Fol - low me in mer - ry meas - ure, Fa la la la la la
la la la, While I tell of Yule - tide trea - sure, Fa la la la la la

la la la.
Fast a-way the old year pass-es, Fa la la la la la
la la la, Hail the new ye lads and lass-es, Fa la la la la la
f

la la la la.
Sing we joy - ous all to - geth - er,
Fa la la la la la la
la la la la la
Heed - less of the wind and - weath - er
Fa la la la la
no ritard.
la la la
la la la.
no ritard.

Flute

# Deck the Hall

Old Welsh Carol
Arranged by Richard Walters

Cut along dotted line.